THE UNIVERSITY OF TEXAS AT TYLER

A
Patriot's
Guide *to*
Success

Words *of* Wisdom
from East Texas Leaders

Published by UT Tyler Press, an imprint of The University of Texas at Tyler.
Printed in the United States of America.

UT Tyler Press
3900 University Blvd.
Tyler, Texas 75799

The University of Texas at
TYLER

Your Success. Our Passion.

TABLE OF CONTENTS

Introduction by Michael Tidwell, PhD
President of University of Texas at Tyler

A
Patriot's
Guide *to*
Success

INTRODUCTION

Michael Tidwell, PhD
President of The University of Texas at Tyler

There are many reasons why students choose to pursue higher education. From a desire to grow intellectually, the drive to become wealthy, the ambition to land a good job or the urge to make a difference in the world, your paths to The University of Texas at Tyler are varied and personal. What binds each of you together is your aspiration to achieve success in life and career!

One of the best ways to ensure success is to seek wise counsel and guidance. This is why *A Patriot's Guide to Success* was assembled. This work represents a compilation of the advice, wisdom and inspirational stories of a diverse group of East Texas leaders. Whether early career professionals or seasoned legends, each leader shares a layer of advocacy and support written to help you determine your path forward.

We all benefit from the wisdom of others. I trust that you will be encouraged and inspired by this volume. ★

JOEL ADAMS
Southside Bank, Executive Vice President

Joel Adams is the executive vice president and program manager for Southside Investment Services. He specializes in helping people with significant life events, such as retirement or receiving an inheritance. He began his career with Southside Bank in 1997 and, in 2018, was named one of the "Top 100 Bank Financial Advisors" in the country by Bank Investment Consultant magazine. The desire to help others is what drove him to the vocation of financial advisor.

Joel is a past regional chairman for the Make-a-Wish Foundation and focuses on serving the needs of the Tyler community through Leadership Tyler and other organizations.

Appreciate Adversity

If there is one point I'd like to drive home it would be how important it is to push through any adversities that arise. Never give up. Ever.

My parents taught me that at an early age and they also taught me the importance of being self-made—of earning something. You never appreciate something that can be obtained easily, and nothing worth having comes cheaply. ★

LARRY ANDERSON, MD/FAAD
U.S. Dermatology Partners of Tyler,
Medical Director

Dr. Larry Anderson is the chief medical officer of U.S. Dermatology Partners, initiating the founding partnership with Dermatology Associates of Tyler in 2013. U.S. Dermatology Partners currently has 300 providers in 94 dermatology practices across eight states.

He is very active in the community, having served on several boards. Through their philanthropic endeavors, he and his wife, Dr. Svetislava Vukelja, have established numerous endowed scholarships at a number of institutions.

The BENEFITS *of* GETTING INVOLVED

The best advice I can offer students is to get involved in something either in the community or on campus. These experiences will provide many opportunities.

Being engaged in campus activities will help you create memories and lifelong friendships.

Getting involved will broaden your circle of friends and expose you to people and ideas to which you might not have experienced otherwise.

It also allows you to experience working together toward a common goal and to develop leadership skills as well as follower skills, which are often more important in today's world. This is knowledge that you might not find in the classroom. Working on a team and with other people is a lifetime skill that you only get with practice.

You will forever remember things you did, people with whom you associated and projects on which you worked.

While the academic information may change over time, the memories will remain the same. ★

JERRY ASHWORTH
TIRR Memorial Hermann Rehabilitation and Research, Senior Vice President and CEO

An accomplished healthcare executive, Jerry Ashworth has more than 25 years of experience in healthcare administration. After joining the leadership team at TIRR Memorial Hermann in 2014, he provided oversight and leadership for hospital operations until his promotion to senior vice president & chief executive officer in March 2018.

Jerry believes strongly in TIRR Memorial Hermann's mission of ensuring independence and inclusion for people with disabilities and is actively involved in creating exceptional patient experiences.

Authentic *and* Open

First, you have to be true to yourself, do not try to be something you are not. Early in my career, someone told me that I needed to change who I was to succeed but I did not take that advice. At the same time, you have to present an image that people trust and believe in. I think it is okay to have a personality and a sense of humor, but people should know that they can count on you; that you are reliable and trustworthy.

Second, it is key to be visible and not be afraid to engage with patients, families, physicians and employees as it helps you connect with people. At the end of the day, we are all human, whether it is a patient or staff member I try to put myself in their shoes and relate to their situation which helps me form a bond with everyone I encounter. ★

JEFF AUSTIN III
Texas Department of Transportation,
Commissioner

Jeff Austin is a seventh generation Texan, a fourth generation banker and currently vice chairman of the board of Austin Bank Texas, NA and Austin Bancorp.

He has served two gubernatorial appointments in the last 14 years. In 2005, he was appointed the first chairman of the North East Texas Regional Mobility Authority (NET RMA) and was reappointed to the position three more times. In 2011, Jeff served in his first appointment as commissioner of the Texas Transportation Commission, which oversees statewide activities of the Texas Department of Transportation. He was reappointed in 2013 for a six-year term.

Jeff is involved with the Texas Bankers' Association, having held positions on the board and committees.

RADAR ON *and* ANTENNA UP

Don't be afraid to ask questions. Don't always be satisfied with the status quo but challenge assumptions respectfully.

Look people in the eye and give a firm handshake. Maintain confidentiality. Be responsive. Write letters sometimes and don't just reply with a text or an email.

Beware of groupthink in decision making. Be an example—you never know who is watching.

Build on your strengths but be aware of your weaknesses. Be strategic—think beyond the first and second move like you are playing chess. And lastly, be observant and a good listener.

In the terms of the Ritz Carlton Leadership training, "Radar on, antenna up!" ★

BARBARA BASS, CPA
Gollob Morgan Peddy PC

Barbara Bass is an officer with Gollob Morgan Peddy—Certified Public Accountants, a large local Tyler firm, and has 35+ years of experience. Her practice focus is on tax planning and accounting needs for small business owners and includes business and personal income tax preparation.

Barbara served as the mayor of Tyler from May 2008 until May 2014. Her service through the Great Recession included innovative and collaborative community initiatives, which poised Tyler for its future growth.

Overnight Success

When asked about her overnight success, my friend clarified by saying, "What overnight success? That was 25 years of hard work!" Think you want to be an overnight success? Then, E.A.R.N. it.

Education – Knowledge, both formal and through life experience, is critical to your success. What are you doing today to get where you want to go tomorrow?

Accountability – Your value system is the foundation of who you are. Setting boundaries and being honest with yourself are part of the framework of who you will become.

Responsibility – Life owes you nothing; you owe it your all. By doing your part, your success will also benefit others—your family, work and community.

Networking – Never stop learning. Life is full of bumps and curves. From hard work to success, life is meant to be shared. Share what you have learned, and learn from what others share.

Still want that overnight success? Enjoy the ride and E.A.R.N. it! ★

GARY BAXTER
G. Baxter Enterprises, CEO

Tyler native Gary Baxter played defensive back for eight years in the NFL—four each with the Baltimore Ravens and the Cleveland Browns.

In 2008, he started G. Baxter Enterprises (GBE), which manages his endeavors in commercial real estate, QSR operations, consulting and sports science medical research. Corporate brands with which GBE is associated are Burger King, Taco Bueno and Project Rose Research Institute for Sports Science.

Chair of the Gary Baxter Foundation, Gary has served on several boards including Baylor Scott & White Health and Wellness Board, NFL Alumni Dallas Chapter, Dallas Center and Helping Restore Ability.

DON'T LET SETBACKS
SET YOU BACK

Challenges and setbacks will come, but see them merely as hurdles that can be overcome. I encourage you to embrace them as learning tools.

Rise up when tough days come upon you. Your ability to navigate tough times will only build character and internal strength preparing you for the next tough time.

Keep a positive attitude at all times no matter what, and keep in mind, no one is immune to adversities in life. Commit to overcoming whatever comes in your path.

Remember, never quit and never give up. ★

CODY BOYD
UT Health East Texas, Division Administrator

Cody Boyd currently serves as the division administrator for cancer services at UT Health East Texas. Cody was born and raised in East Texas and found his way back after a seven-year business venture that helped his family capitalize on traveling opportunities.

While living in Fort Worth, the Boyds set out on an adventure that combined a consulting/contracting business with a love for travel. This exposed Cody to a multitude of healthcare settings and the opportunity to utilize those acquired and inherent skills to help create a new oncology practice at what is now the UT Health North Campus Tyler MD Anderson Cancer Center.

The DOORS *of* LIFE

I have found that life is full of doors. Some doors are closed and we find ourselves wondering what lies behind them. Other doors are open, and this is where I choose to focus my thoughts. My greatest successes and most valuable lessons have been a result of when I've jumped through open doors.

Many times, I've wondered what I've gotten myself into, but ultimately these experiences have shaped my career and fueled my passion to do more. If you don't walk through open doors, someone else will.

Stay focused. Stay determined. Stay hungry. ★

BRIAN BRANDT
Core Insights, CEO

Brian Brandt is CEO of Core Insights, a Texas based company that provides training, strategic planning, coaching and a speakers bureau. He holds a master's degree in global leadership and a bachelor's degree in accounting. Based on his 30 years of leadership experience, he regularly speaks and writes on a variety of leadership, communication and organizational topics.

A Moment *of* Reflection

As you consider your future, take some time to process your past. Ask yourself questions like:

- What do I naturally do well?
- What do people consistently ask me to help them with?
- What do I tend to do at a higher level than my peers?
- What do I really care about?
- What kind of work do I enjoy doing?
- What frustrates me?
- THEN, ask yourself – What would I like life to look like in five years?

The responses to these questions can provide great insights into what opportunities we should seek to create. Additionally, these answers can shape what we say "yes" and what we say "no" to. Typically, the ways we get from our current situation to our desired state is through education, relationships and experience. So, reflect on your past, contemplate your future and move forward deliberately. ★

BRAD BROOKSHIRE
Brookshire Grocery Co., Chairman and CEO

Brad Brookshire has served as chairman of the board of directors since 2007 and as chief executive officer since 2015. He has more than 40 years of leadership with the company and serves on the board of directors for the Food Marketing Institute and Topco Associates. He also serves on the board of trustees for Southern Methodist University and the Baylor Hospital Foundation board.

Brookshire's is a family business that was established in Tyler in 1928 on a strong foundation of service, integrity and excellence that still drives actions and decisions today. The company is committed to the causes of hunger relief, education, family well-being and honoring first responders and military heroes in communities that support Brookshire's, Super 1 Foods, Spring Market and FRESH by Brookshire's stores.

THREE THINGS *to* REMEMBER

There are three pieces of advice that apply regardless of your stage in life.

1. Have courage in the face of adversity. Hard times come and go. It's important to stay focused on your goals and not become distracted by the obstacles. Those who persevere and stay the course will come out stronger on the other side.

2. Choose your friends wisely. Surround yourself with positive people whose values and character you admire and respect.

3. Dedicate yourself to lifelong learning. A college degree is just the first step. Developing to your full potential takes a lifetime of stretching yourself in every aspect of life.

I have learned many lessons during the past 42 years in the grocery business. None are more significant than standing strong when the going gets tough, surrounding yourself with great people and learning something new every day. ★

KIRK A. CALHOUN, MD/FACP
The University of Texas Health Science Center at Tyler, President

Dr. Kirk Calhoun is president of UT Health Science Center at Tyler, the only academic medical center in Northeast Texas, and chairman of the board of UT Health East Texas Health System. Through a partnership between UT Health Science Center at Tyler and Ardent Services, this newly formed health system owns and operates 10 hospitals, 50-plus clinics, emergency transport services, a home health agency and other health related enterprises.

STAY *the* COURSE

College is a unique time in one's life. This era lends to self-discovery, change, formulation of new ideas and thought processes, and ultimately, setting a trajectory for future success. Going to college is not easy; obtaining a degree is not easy. You will be expected to make pivotal decisions about your future, to establish a career path, work toward it and complete the complex task of obtaining a college degree.

These goals require a mindset and the determination that you will succeed. It requires perseverance and an unwavering commitment to your future. Stay focused on your dreams and goals—persevere. When things become difficult, as they undoubtedly will, stay the course. You will be tired, but persevere. Engage with your peers, lean on your support staff, build relationships and, most importantly, finish. In the end, when you receive your degree, you will have earned it. ★

JACKIE CANNON
Champions for Children, Executive Director

Jackie Cannon, the executive director of Champions for Children for the last five years, is a retired educator, with 26 years of experience serving as a classroom teacher, instructional specialist and assistant principal.

Jackie holds a bachelor's degree in counseling and a master's degree in education as well as reading specialist and principal certifications. She is active in the community and is dedicated to sharing the mission of Champions for Children with Smith County and beyond.

Extracurricular Opportunities

Extracurricular life in college is so important for future success and networking. I had the opportunity to put myself through college and had very little extracurricular life. As I look back, I would have joined more organizations, been involved in more leadership events and attended more school-related functions. I would have explored financial aid options so that I could work less and be more engaged in campus life.

As a result, I encouraged my children to be engaged in campus activities. They participated in college sports, student government, fraternity extracurricular, football and as a student trainer and freshman mentor. They developed valuable skills in leadership, teamwork and networking.

I realize that had I been more involved, when I graduated, I would have had a network of friends and acquaintances with whom I could consult about issues or problems and with whom I could socialize professionally.

Currently, UT Tyler has more than 80 student organizations of which you can be a part. I encourage you to get involved. Build relationships, lifelong friends and contacts. ★

CHARLIE CANO
Etex Communications,
General Manager and CEO

Charlie Cano is a veteran of the telecom industry. His diverse work experience includes working as an outside plant design engineer, a project manager and director of sales for a national consulting firm.

Working with companies of all sizes, Charlie specialized in engineering and strategic planning. Since 2003, he has been applying his leadership and technical knowledge and guiding Etex Communications to the deployment of business and residential phones, internet, Wi-Fi and all new telecommunication advanced services.

Charlie implements a focus on culture, the latest in technology and excellence in customer support to drive success.

THE FORMULA

$$VF = \int_{HD}^{R} \frac{(P + G^2 + GR)}{R\,t\,C}$$

A successful person's value comes from realizing that the professional focus should be constant from beginning to end—from the day you are hired through retirement. Once hired, three things develop your success.

First, we all graduate with a skill that translates to our work performance. It is what you bring to the table.

Add to that a double dose of grit, which is the fire (your background, challenges, motivators) that inspires you to get an education and evolve. Everyone has a story, something that inspires us to the next level. Grit also represents your potential to grow. We are never done learning.

A significant companion to grit is treating your fellow man with respect, honor and integrity. That goes a long way, both at the beginning and end of a career.

Finally, understand that the person you are today will not be the same in the future, and you don't want to be. Do not resist change, for it will decrease your entire value factor. ★

$$Value\ Factor = \int_{Hire\ Date}^{Retirement} \frac{Performance + Grit^2 + Golden\ Rule}{Resistance\ to\ Change}$$

JOHN P. CARR
Carr Resources Inc., President

John Carr developed as a geologist with Delta Drilling Co. As Delta was going public he moved to work with a group of geophysicists at Power Exploration. Having absorbed a good deal of geophysical knowledge, he moved to a start-up exploration and production company with Jim Rippy at Sunnybrook Oil and Gas. John continued there until the company was sold in 1984 and he started his own company, which has run in different iterations since that time.

John graduated from the Episcopal Iona School for Ministry in 2012 and was ordained into the priesthood January 15, 2016.

COURAGE

The four classical cardinal virtues—prudence, justice, temperance and courage—are important for success, but courage is essential to a successful business life.

That is, the courage to always tell the truth, the courage not to compromise your standards, the courage to lead while others fall back, the courage to stand up for the truth in all situations. Courage is essential.

The three theological virtues of faith, hope and charity might seem out of place in a business discussion but they, too, are vital.

Faith is needed when everyone wants to quit. Hope is essential when everyone is discouraged. Charity, or love, based on mutual respect, is needed at all times whether closing a deal, building a team or leading employees.

Your courage will build your reputation as a dependable person who always tells the truth, respects others and deals fairly with competitors and partners alike. ★

MOODY CHISHOLM
UT Health East Texas, President and CEO

Moody Chisholm is responsible for the extensive operations of UT Health East Texas, which includes 10 hospitals, more than 50 clinics, two freestanding emergency centers, regional rehabilitation facilities and home health services, a comprehensive seven-trauma center care network—including a Level 1—and a fleet of more than 45 ambulances and four helicopters.

A FOUNDATION *of* TRUST

S ome of the best advice I've learned over the course
of my career comes from Patrick Lencioni's *The Five
Dysfunctions of a Team* and the belief that trust is at the
core of all relationships.

The dysfunctions preventing effective teamwork can be
laid out in the shape of a pyramid, each layer contributing
to the next. At the base—the foundation of the five
dysfunctions—is absence of trust.

In order to be successful in work and in life, we
must have trust—in ourselves and in others. A big part
of developing trust as a leader is showing your own
vulnerability so that others feel safe to show vulnerability.
Putting on a facade that you never make mistakes is not
going to encourage vulnerability and trust. Being open
about your own errors will show that it is OK to make
mistakes, and it will encourage the mindset that sharing
opposing views is the best path to success. ★

MIKE COBB
All Saints Episcopal School, Head of School

Mike Cobb has served schools as a teacher, coach, division head, admissions director and head of school for over 20 years.

His passion for student engagement and authentic learning has led him into creating numerous programs and spaces centered on 1:1 Ed, makerspaces and 21st Century Leadership. Mike has led extensive training for administrators in innovative practices for school leaders looking to thrive in the future.

CONSTRUCTING SUCCESS

The idea of success is a personal pondering and one that is defined by each person individually. The journey to a successful life follows a path that is not straight but rather takes turns and dives. We must embrace the fact that we are always "under construction" and should be in pursuit of experiencing joy in our life.

Indeed, John Dewey said more than 100 years ago that education is a process of living, and not a preparation for the future living. It is the trend in our world today to desire "instant gratification" and to mark success with a check mark in the done category.

However, I think we have to be bold and accept that there is no "done" category in becoming a leader for tomorrow. Our journey is one that takes us into uncharted areas on a daily basis. After all, we are all under construction. ★

DAVID COBLE
City of Tyler, Fire Chief

David Coble is the managing director of emergency services for the city of Tyler. He serves as the emergency management coordinator as well as the fire chief.

He began his public service career in 1984 as a firefighter and successfully advanced through the ranks. In 2013, he served as executive assistant chief of the 16th largest city before accepting his current position in Tyler.

PERSEVERANCE

I succeed by continuing to persevere in the face of adversity. Originally, I was a commuter student in college. I stayed home and drove back and forth to college every day.

After my parents moved away, I was on my own to handle all of my living and college expenses. After my $2,500 scholarship ran out, I paid my own way through graduate school. I never had a loan and had no student debt.

For me, it is about not letting any obstacle get in the way of reaching your goal. ★

DANIEL CRAWFORD, EdD
Robert E. Lee High School, Principal

Dr. Daniel Crawford has been a campus administrator for 16 years and is serving in his 13th year as a campus principal. He has served in urban, suburban and rural school districts, and has worked in five different classifications of schools, from the 2A to 6A level.

He is currently in his fourth year as principal at Robert E. Lee High School in Tyler, which has approximately 2,200 students.

Big-Picture Thinking

Successful leaders spend their time questioning both what they know and don't know.

When you question, you gain knowledge, and when you gain knowledge, you have an impact. Successful leaders also know the key to being impactful is to question what everyone else takes for granted, which will give you an advantage in terms of innovation and creativity.

These individuals are also big-picture thinkers who are always ready and embrace the opportunity to see what others cannot see. They accomplish this by taking into account all available variables when sizing up a situation. Once you can connect the dots like no one else, you are ready to seize an opportunity when the time is right. Successful leaders think big and dream even bigger than most others dream. ★

WHITNEY CREWS
Lindale ISD Teacher,
2015 Texas Elementary Teacher of the Year

Whitney Crews is a 23-year educator, almost entirely as a sixth grade teacher in Lindale ISD. The 2019–20 school year brings a new adventure as the fourth-sixth grade gifted and talented teacher at the same campus. The Texas Association of School Administrators selected her as the 2015 Texas Elementary Teacher of the Year.

As a member of the National Network of State Teachers of the Year, she serves on the membership committee, presented at their national conference and contributed to Teaching Partners' 100 Ways online professional development project.

Ahead *of the* Game

I f you are actually reading this book shortly after receiving it instead of 20 years later, then you are already way ahead of the game.

The first step to success is to acknowledge that those around you possess a wealth of wisdom gained from a unique combination of experiences; and then, you must be willing to learn from them.

As a 23-year veteran teacher, my experience has taught me to surround yourself with people who are where you want to be and who challenge you to be better instead of just maintaining status quo.

Ann Landers said, "Opportunities are usually disguised as hard work; so most people don't recognize them." Taking on a task someone else passes on often opens a door for you that remains locked to others. ★

KEVIN ELTIFE
The University of Texas System Board of Regents, Chairman

Kevin Eltife was appointed to a six-year term on The University of Texas System Board of Regents by Governor Greg Abbott in January 2017 and was confirmed by the Texas Senate on February 7, 2017.

In 2018, Kevin was elected chairman of the Board of Regents. He chairs the System Review and Structure Task Force and previously served on the Academic Affairs Committee; Audit, Compliance and Risk Management Committee; Facilities Planning and Construction Committee; Finance and Planning Committee; and the Board for Lease of University Lands.

He served as District 1 Texas senator, mayor of Tyler and a member of the Tyler City Council and Texas Higher Education Coordinating Board.

Two Things Mother Taught Me

My father died when I was one and half years old. My mother was left with three children ages one, five and nine, and she dedicated the rest of her life to raising us to understand two things:

1. There are always those who are less fortunate, and we should do everything we can to help them and treat them with respect.
2. The key to success is education.

She encouraged us to find our passion and live life with honesty, kindness and integrity. The best advice I can give anyone is this same advice my mother gave to me. ★

JAY FERGUSON, EdD
Grace Community School, Head of School

Dr. Jay Ferguson has been head of school for Grace Community School, the largest private school in East Texas, for almost 20 years.

He was a practicing attorney for 10 years before joining Grace in 2002 as its director of development. In 2003, he became the head of school. Since that time, he has worked to develop a "whole ministry" approach for Grace Community School through a unified relationship between the upper and lower campuses, and a strengthened bond between church and school.

GIFT *of* HUMILITY

Humility is the gateway to greatness, which is exactly the opposite of the way we think the world works. We think that if you're prideful—you strut your stuff, you show off—then you become great. But, it really doesn't work that way at all. Pride is actually the engine of mediocrity. It convinces you that you're better than you think you really are, so you never actually become as good as you can be.

Paradoxically, humility removes the shallow lid from your life, allowing life to pour in empathy, compassion, love, understanding, excellence, wisdom, intelligence and all the great stuff that makes this life worth living.

So, here's the thing: We can't become humble by willing ourselves to be humble. There is no humility without humiliation. Difficult circumstances are the mechanisms of humility.

When challenges come, people of pride curse their circumstances, while humble people accept the difficulties as painful yet precious gifts that will make them stronger.

Never be afraid of humility. Embrace it. ★

MITCH FORTNER, PE
KSA, President

Mitch Fortner is leading KSA with 35 years of experience in the industry.

A professional engineer in Texas since 1988, Mitch's career has been widely varied and has involved engineering design, construction administration and project management on airports, water systems, wastewater systems, streets and drainage, parks, industrial facilities, and many other types of projects.

Since joining KSA, he has served as design engineer, project engineer, project manager, division manager, director of marketing, executive vice president and now president.

READ *to* LEAD

Learn to love reading. It is very true that leaders read and readers lead. Read about leaders in the field that you choose to join. If you are pursuing a career in business, read about the great business minds.

You can benefit by learning from the hard-earned life experiences of those who came before you.

Do not think too highly of your knowledge, and always take time to listen to the voices of wisdom from people around you. ★

DAWN FRANKS
Your Philanthropy, President

Dawn Franks, president and CEO of Your Philanthropy, a coaching and consulting firm, works with donors, private foundations and the nonprofit community. She has 38 years of experience working with nonprofits and donors across the country. She oversees grant-making activities for five family foundations and consults with them on a range of issues.

In her early nonprofit career, she co-founded the East Texas Crisis Center, serving as the executive director for 15 years, and later served as CEO of the United Way of Smith County. Dawn spent 13 years with the Fourth Partner Foundation, a giving intermediary.

Dawn is the author of *Giving Fingerprints,* an e-book that's available at her site your-philanthropy.com.

WHAT'S NEXT?

The questions that loom large as you navigate a college education are: What's next? What career, what advanced degree, where to start?

I had all the same questions and was surprised to discover what was next as opportunities presented themselves in my last semester.

A professor encouraged me to write on a particular topic, and that led to research and new relationships that developed into a job opportunity. I didn't have exactly the right degree, but that led me to continue learning and add more education. I realized I was on exactly the right career track as the years passed.

When opportunities come that allow you to broaden your horizons in unexpected directions, take them. The path ahead is seldom visible; take the next few steps clearly in front of you. Count as gain all opportunities to learn and experience along the way. ★

BOB GARRETT
Fair Oil Company, President

Bob Garrett is president and CEO of Fair Oil Co., a Tyler-based oil and gas exploration company established in 1931. A real estate developer, Bob has served as president of the Tyler Area Builders Association and the Texas Association of Builders, which named him Developer of the Year in 2007.

Bob has long been active in civic affairs including the Tyler Economic Development Council, where he served for 15 years; Meadows Mental Health Policy Institute; Salvation Army Development Board; and the boards of Southside Bank and T. B. Butler Publishing Co.

A COUPLE *of* THINGS *to* CONSIDER

Talent is a gift, character is a choice (John C. Maxwell). One who possesses character strives to do what is right. It is not because of the rule of law, but because of the self-realization that our principle responsibility as citizens is to do the right thing, treat others with respect and produce more than we consume.

We can neither write nor enforce enough law to replace this principle and, without it, simple talent becomes useless over time. Be a person of character!

Try not to become a person of success but rather a person of value (Albert Einstein). Don't spend your life measuring the impact that your actions have on yourself, rather, spend your life measuring the impact that you have on others. ★

ROCKY GILL
Express Employment Professionals, Owner

Rocky Gill opened Express Employment Professionals in Tyler in 1995. His goal continues to be providing the best staffing services available to East Texas.

The Tyler office has been honored as a Circle of Excellence every year since 1998. The last several years, the Tyler office has been included in the Chairman's Club, recognizing the top 10 offices out of nearly 800.

Focus, Character *and* Passion

Every person has their own definition of success. You're no exception. In terms of your career, I'd like to propose that you consider these three things:

First, focus on how you can bring value to a company. Start that conversation in the interview. Postpone discussing what you want or need from the job. Find out how you can contribute to their success.

Second, read Patrick Lencioni's book *The Ideal Team Player* and develop the character traits humble, hungry and smart. Better yet, become that person!

Finally, find work that energizes you. In every job, there are parts that are simply work. But there should be at least 20 percent of any job where time flies because you love it so much and you're having fun. Find a job that gives you that 20 percent!

If you must work to support yourself, you might as well be successful. Often, the amount of extra long-term energy required for success is not that much more than being mediocre. Go for success! ★

PAUL L. GLEISER
KTBB Radio, President

Paul Gleiser is a lifelong radio broadcaster who owns three radio stations serving the Tyler/Longview area.

IT's *as* SIMPLE *as* THIS...

When people like me are asked to contribute to a project like this, the nearly overwhelming temptation is to give big-picture advice from high atop some mountain. I'm going to resist that temptation.

Here is advice from street level that is about as "small picture" as you can get. Yet if you follow it, it will yield *huge* results.

Answer phone calls, return phone calls and send handwritten thank-you notes.

I *guarantee* that you will stand out. Almost nobody does these things anymore. When you do, it *will* be noticed in a way that works to your distinct advantage.

For a few dollars, you can go to any number of websites and order personalized note cards. Do it. And then use them—every time someone does something that helps you.

And try to never let the sun set on an unreturned phone call. Make this a habit and somewhere along the way in your career, you'll thank me. ★

THE HONORABLE JUDITH GUTHRIE
United States District Court, Retired Judge

Judith Guthrie retired in 2013 after 27 years as a United States magistrate judge in the Eastern District of Texas.

She began her legal career with the Bracewell Law Firm from 1975 until 1981 when she took a leave of absence to clerk for the chief judge of the Court of Appeals in Tyler. Instead of returning to Houston after her clerkship, Judith formed a partnership with her late husband John Hannah (Hannah & Guthrie) and was in private practice until her judicial appointment in 1986.

It *is* Good *to* Have *a* Plan, But...

My best advice for you at this point is to make a very general plan to meet a goal you have set for yourself. Hopefully the goal will start with finishing college and getting a degree in a subject area you find interesting.

Once you have finished college, if you still don't know what you want to be, then my advice is to pick a place where you would like to live and move there. When you get there, find a job, any job, so that you can afford to stay there awhile. Try going to an employment agency for temporary work. Then you will have time to search for the perfect job.

In the meantime, you will wake up happy every morning to be living in a place you like. ★

KATHERINE HARTVICKSON
Quantum Ascendance, President

Katherine Hartvickson is a human resources consultant, leadership expert, speaker, author, trainer and coach.

She is president of Quantum Ascendance, an HR and leadership development consulting firm that has been helping small to mid-size businesses, organizations, teams and individuals reach their potential since 2010. Katherine's passion is growing and equipping business owners to achieve remarkable heights as well as systematize and prioritize their business challenges when it comes to getting the best from their team.

A FEW STEPS *to* SUCCESS

Looking back over my career, several things contributed to my success. Here are a few most relevant to where you are today:

- Invest in yourself, know yourself authentically, identify your passion and create your life blueprint.
- Obtain a degree aligned with your passion so that it will support you spiritually, emotionally and economically.
- Learn from personal development books and from leaders you admire.
- Surround yourself with people who exude positive energy, have goals and are successful. They will inspire you to achieve more.
- Dress for the job you want.

A senior executive who was upset with me over an employee-privacy issue once told me that I wouldn't go very far because my nails were too long and my lipstick was too bright. I've often wondered what he thinks now, knowing I have achieved executive status in global organizations, own a consulting business and wrote two best-selling books. Don't listen to the naysayers. ★

BRIAN HAYS
Patriot Food Delivery, Owner and Founder

Brian Hays graduated from UT Tyler with a Bachelor of Science in industrial technology.

In late 2013, he saw an emerging industry in restaurant/food delivery and co-founded Patriot Restaurant Delivery to help students and others have access to online or app based ordering from their favorite local restaurants.

Since inception, the business and industry has grown exponentially and they have been voted the #1 Locally Loved Service for three years straight.

Brian is also the founder/operator of Loyal Logistics and co-founder of Northeast Properties.

He is married to his high school sweetheart Tara Hays and they have two kids Hannah and Barron.

You Determine Your Success!

It starts with a vision and goals. Always remember, many times true conviction and passion can lead to outcomes that were previously believed to be unrealistic.

Dream big, believe in what you are doing, be focused and understand that persistence is key. Giving up should never be an option.

If you work hard, be nice and truly care, you will be amazed by how far that will get you.

Seek guidance from God and wise elders who already understand and have lived what you need to know.

Lastly, have good intentions in everything you do and build a good foundation. Know what you believe, why you believe it and don't let anyone tell you that your vision isn't attainable.

That is the Patriot mindset. ★

THE HONORABLE MARTIN HEINES
City of Tyler, Mayor

Mayor Martin Heines is a small business owner and property manager and investor. He served two terms as Tyler city councilman for District 4, before becoming mayor in 2014.

His involvement in the community has been diverse, serving the city of Tyler as a volunteer on several committees including the International Existing Building Code Committee, which he chaired; the Steering Committee for Tyler 1st; Mayor's Tyler Leadership Roundtable; and Midtown Area Development Committee.

NOT JUST ONE THING

The best advice I can give any young person coming of age in this economy is not to pigeonhole yourself into thinking you will do, and therefore be, only one thing.

It has been true for me, and will be especially true for you, that you will have the opportunity to have several careers, if that is what you want. The sooner you take your blinders off and start thinking beyond your education track, you will see all the opportunities available to you.

Look around and you will see there has never been a better time to be in business for yourself. New technologies and automation give you opportunities to be at the forefront of entirely new fields. Don't be afraid to try something no one has ever done before—that is innovation. If you don't see the job you want in the market today, why not create it?

Finally, don't forget to give back to the communities that are home to you and your business. ★

BILLY HIBBS
Heartland Security Insurance Group,
Chairman and CEO

Billy Hibbs leads a family business that is one of the largest insurance holding companies in the southwest, as well as one of the nation's largest providers of claims services to the federal government. Heartland Security Insurance Group is a diversified organization comprised of eight individual companies, including a technology business. Each of the companies offers solutions to distinct client groups who need insurance and risk management services.

This attitude toward service extends to a multitude of philanthropic and educational causes that are supported across the community and around the world.

THE SECRET SAUCE

Some 30 years ago, I was the CFO for a family business in Dallas. Before meals, the owner would offer a prayer for the families he employed, as well as the business, even when we dined at restaurants. This made a lasting impression on me. I watched as his business was blessed, particularly during the severe depression that gripped Texas during much of the 1980s.

After joining our family insurance and risk management business, now known as Heartland Security Insurance Group, we began opening every board meeting, every investment committee meeting and every luncheon with prayer. It's so important to our culture that our corporate minutes record *who offers the prayer*. Like my prior employer, we have been extraordinarily blessed even during challenging economic periods.

What is the "secret sauce" that has enabled us to thrive for over half a century?

Prayer is underrated as a business strategy. ★

GAYLORD HUGHEY JR.
Attorney

Most of Gaylord Hughey's time is currently allocated to various governmental relations activities in a myriad of subject matters ranging from Homeland Security, International Trade Commission, patent reform, construction, oil and gas, tax reform, healthcare, social media, regulatory reform, trade, and commerce. His passions are the development and implementation of strategies to solve complex problems and the formulating of public policy at the local, state and federal levels.

Trusted Relationships

Develop trusted relationships. They are few and far between, particularly in the workplace. They are earned with time and performance.

The significance of trusted relationships is that they allow you to utilize your discretion based upon shared values to address the circumstances before you. Trusted relationships are time efficient and empowering in the context of solving problems. You are not only representing your interests but also those who have entrusted you to represent their interests.

Trusted relationships within a diversified skill network have yielded opportunities beyond what I could have otherwise identified for all parties involved. The ability to engage trusted relationships provides input and resources to implement a broad range of business plans once that opportunity is identified. Grow your network, nurture it and be empowered as you develop and embrace your trusted relationships. ★

CARRIE-ANN JASPER-YEARTY
Jasper Ventures Inc., Vice President of People

Carrie-Ann Jasper-Yearty currently serves as vice president of people for Jasper Ventures Inc. and affiliated companies.

She joined the team in 2011 as the business manager for EPC Inc., and in 2016, she returned to her human resources roots, taking the role of vice president of human resources for the reorganized company Jasper Ventures Inc.

Prior to joining the family business, she spent the first 16 years of her career in human resources management in manufacturing, financial services and banking.

Cultivate Relationships

When I transitioned from my undergraduate studies at UT Tyler into my career, the pivotal moment for me was about a year after my graduation.

I received a call from a UT Tyler professor, to whom I had made it clear that I desired a career in human resources. When a local company came looking for HR candidates, he recalled our conversations and reached out to me, putting me in contact with the company.

If I had not had a relationship with my professor where I shared this information, I would not have had the opportunity to work in the field I desired. Follow your passion and find a career that you love, but make sure you cultivate the right relationships along the way. ★

JONATHAN JONES
Jonathan Jones Speaks, Amazon Bestselling Author and TedX Speaker

Jonathan Jones serves and supports millennial entrepreneurs who believe in self-investing, monetizing their message and leaving a legacy.

He has been featured on CBS News and has spoken to thousands of students ranging from elementary school to college. He is the host of the Speak Your Success podcast and the author of *Process: 14 Surprisingly Simple Behaviors to Skyrocket Millennials to Success*.

Ready *vs.* Prepared

Understand the difference between being ready and being prepared. Students are ready to graduate and go into the real world to live their professional lives, but sometimes they are not prepared.

Make sure you have done the necessary research on your career of choice.

- Polish your resume.
- Practice your communication skills so that you successfully interview.

Once you get the job, identify a mentor who can guide you through the challenges of the position. Concentrate on your professional development so that you will become a driving force in the workplace. ★

DAVID KING
Primoris Services Corp., Chairman and CEO

David King is the chairman and CEO of Primoris Services Corp., which is a $3.5 billion organization with more than 12,000 employees nationwide. He oversees the strategic and financial directions of the organization.

His illustrious career also includes leadership roles for very reputable engineering companies including Howe-Baker International and Chicago Bridge & Iron.

What's *the* Endgame?

Although I have no regrets, if I had my collegiate experience to do over, I would slow down and relish it more.

Even though I was very active on campus, I felt at that time the endgame was a career. I was in a rush to get out of college and start working. I should have realized that I was already in the game. What I also should have realized was there is no endgame. The game continues until we leave this earth.

The collegiate experience is not separate from your career. It is a vital part of it. ★

KIMBERLY LEWIS
Goodwill Industries of East Texas,
President and CEO

Kimberly Lewis has more than 19 years of executive level nonprofit and business experience. As president of Goodwill Industries of East Texas, she has implemented a reentry program for ex-offenders; veterans training program; workplace literacy program in partnership with the Literacy Council of Tyler; Good Assist, a benefits assistance program in partnership with the East Texas Foodbank; and Youthworks Academy for Out of School Youth.

Under her leadership Goodwill Industries of East Texas received the 2019 and 2017 Center of Excellence Award from Goodwill Industries International and the 2017 Impact Award from the East Texas Human Needs Network.

Kimberly just published her second book titled, *A Seat at the Table or a Part of the Meal.*

MAKE TIME MATTER

When I entered college, I was excited, nervous, energetic and exhausted, all at the same time. I was not sure about what my future held, but that was okay.

College is a time to explore new subjects and broaden your thinking. I encourage you to envision yourself higher, contributing to the world as only YOU can. Everything you need is already inside of you.

This time of serious study will reveal the talents you possess. Pay attention to the things that make your heart sing, and to the things that bother you to the point that you must change them – therein lies your purpose. It's easy to make a dollar; it's hard to make a difference. Making a difference requires an investment. The investment of an education is never a waste of time; it is just the beginning of making your time matter. ★

MICHAEL MCCLENDON
Sages Vintage and Kiepersol Enterprises, Partner and Winemaker

Graduating from Van High School and then from The University of Texas at Tyler as a Faulconer Scholar, Michael McClendon is an enologist and winemaker. His career has taken him all over the world from Chile to New Zealand. In 2017 Michael co-founded Sages Vintage Custom Crush Winery in Nacogdoches, Texas.

McClendon has been featured in the Tyler Loop, Edible Houston, and is even a part of the permanent collection in the Tyler Museum of Art.

Stay Hungry

They say the wolf on the hill is never as hungry as the wolf climbing the hill.

I like to use motivation to drive me. A big mantra that I've adhered to is to stay hungry.

In your undergraduate career, you're going to be on a college campus for the first time. The competition to be accepted to school is over and you'll feel a tendency to lose your killer instinct and relax.

Don't do it!

Stay hungry and put in the work during those first few years, when graduating seems a lifetime away. The same will hold true as you complete your degree. It might be tempting to say, "Look, I have a job now and I'm an adult." I implore you to stay hungry for more, for better.

Be a wolf; enjoy the thrill of the hunt. ★

MICHAEL J. MCNALLY
McNally & Patrick, LLP, Partner

Michael McNally is a partner in the Tyler, Texas law firm of McNally & Patrick, LLP. He has been selected on multiple occasions by his peers as a "Texas Super Lawyer" and was recently honored by the Smith County Bar Foundation with its annual Justinian Award, recognizing lifetime professional achievement coupled with service to both the profession and the community.

Be Opportunistic, Adaptive *and* Bold

Bill and Bob met as college freshmen in 1963. After graduation, Bill was called to military service. He took the opportunity for pilot training which led to a long career as a commercial airline pilot where he seized an opportunity to lead the pilots' union. Upon retirement from the cockpit, he utilized his experience as a pilot and a labor representative to become a highly paid mediator of labor-management conflicts in the airline industry.

Bob took his architecture degree to a large architectural firm that designed major office buildings. In listening to the firm's clients, he realized that while his firm focused on the form and fashion of their exterior designs, the clients were more interested in the interior spaces where they would be working. At the time, the creative design of interior space was largely neglected by the profession. He saw the need, left his secure job and started a firm specializing in interior architecture. His firm now maintains offices around the world.

To maximize the value of your degree, you must be opportunistic, adaptive and bold. ★

CHRISTOPHER MORAN, EdD
Whitehouse ISD, Superintendent

Dr. Christopher Moran is in his 27th year in public education and has been blessed to serve as teacher, coach, bus driver, assistant principal, high school principal and, now, superintendent, a position he has held for the last eight years.

He also serves on the Texas Education Agency Commissioner's Cabinet and is a Texas Association of School Administrators mentor for new superintendents.

The JOYS *of* TEACHING

In this life, you will win and lose by the way you choose. Public education is the key to preparing our next generation to choose wisely and lead effectively. The need for schoolteachers across Texas is critical, and the merit the teaching profession provides is immeasurable.

Mark Twain tells us, "The two most important days in your life are the day you are born and the day you find out why."

Teaching is a wonderful career choice for individuals interested in a rewarding career and an opportunity to mold lives. UT Tyler prepared me well to be an effective public school educator, and my life is filled with the joy and wonder of working with students and staff daily. Each day I give it my best, pray that it is blessed and let God take care of the rest. ★

THE HONORABLE NATHANIEL MORAN
Smith County, Texas, County Judge

Judge Nathaniel Moran is an attorney who has wide-ranging experience, including in the areas of business and commercial litigation and transaction work.

As county judge of Smith County, Judge Moran presides over the five-member commissioners court and handles a wide range of county matters. His responsibilities include acting as budget officer of the county, chairman of the Smith County Juvenile Board, presiding officer of the Smith County Commissioners Court, head of emergency management and the chief administrative officer for the departments overseen by the commissioners court. Additionally, Judge Moran is the presiding judge over the constitutional county court, which has original judicial jurisdiction over probate, guardianship and mental health case files in Smith County.

Rights *and* Responsibilities

In large measure, success in life is a result of choosing the right set of principles, setting the right priorities and then steadily making each decision (large and small) based on the worldview created by those principles and priorities.

My worldview is driven by the principles and priorities interwoven in the natural law of God.

Regardless of your worldview, at some point, you will have to choose how to prioritize between a focus on your rights and your responsibilities. I urge you to choose the latter.

When a person is focused on their responsibilities, they become hard-working, determined, productive, without excuse, selfless, giving and a defender of the rights of others. Conversely, when a person is focused on their rights, they become distracted, jealous, excuse-ridden, bitter, lazy and a thief of the rights of others. Only one path leads to individual success and a life of fulfillment.

Be responsibility-focused! ★

THOMAS G. MULLINS
Tyler Economic Development Council,
President and CEO

Thomas Mullins is also president and CEO of the Tyler Area Chamber of Commerce.

Under his leadership, Tyler Economic Development Council (TEDC) became the first economic development organization in Texas to be an Accredited Economic Development Organization (AEDO) by the International Economic Development Council (IEDC). Including TEDC, there are nine AEDOs in Texas and 44 in North America (as of September 2015).

Work Hard *and* Be *the* Best

My advice to UT Tyler students, especially to those who are just beginning their college experience, is to take it one day, one week, one month at a time.

I came from a poor family with a single mother who never allowed us to stop working hard and being the best we could be every day. That approach to life has served me well. ★

YAZIRI ORROSTIETA
WorkHub, CEO

Yaziri Orrostieta previously served as the marketing director for Heritage Land Bank and marketing manager for Mentoring Minds. Throughout her career, Yaziri has successfully led initiatives in various marketing channels such as direct mail, event marketing, web development and public relations.

She is also a real estate entrepreneur and has over five years experience in retail banking and lending.

Be Open *to* New Opportunities, Get Involved

D o not be afraid to get involved, even when it is not your field of study or area of interest. As a student, this is your time to explore different things and develop, or pursue, passions that may turn into a career.

When I was a UT Tyler student majoring in marketing, I joined the Financial Management Association because they were willing to let me do their advertising and marketing. Even though the organization was outside my area of study, I developed marketing skills as a result of that experience.

After graduating, I took a position at Heritage Land Bank, and while I had no experience in agriculture, I knew how to handle marketing. Had I not gotten involved in something in which I had no experience, I would not have taken this opportunity in agriculture that gave me a career, not just a job.

When I took my new position as CEO of WorkHub, I was nervous about doing something new, but past experiences led me to let go of any fear and give it my all. ★

NANCY RANGEL
Tyler Hispanic Business Alliance,
President and CEO

Nancy Rangel has been an integral part of the continued success of the Tyler Hispanic Business Alliance. Her passion, leadership, organizational and strategic planning skills have assisted the Tyler HBA during its initial transition years of its formation to a 501c3/nonprofit status, and she has remained the thriving force behind its continued growth and success.

Nancy is actively involved in leadership positions with both state and local professional organizations.

The JOURNEY

Throughout my journey in life, there have been many lessons, seasons and experiences that I have learned to navigate.

Remember that life is a journey not a destination. There will be many ups and downs but never be afraid of a storm. A storm will serve as an opportunity for you to learn how to sail to your next destination.

In the end, whatever you decide to do, always be your best, do your best and continually learn from those around you. ★

WHIT RITER
A.W. Riter Jr. Family Foundation;
Riter Management Co., President

Whit Riter is president of Riter Management Co. LC and the A.W. Riter Jr. Family Foundation. Riter Management Co. LC is a privately owned company that manages all of the business and investment activities for the Riter family entities. The A.W. Riter Jr. Family Foundation is a private family foundation whose mission is to glorify God by providing tangible support to those whose work is transforming lives in the community. He also is chief financial officer for iDesign, an education technology company founded by his son.

Whit has served a gubernatorial appointment to the Texas Higher Education Coordinating Board, where he was chair for two years as well as a member of several committees.

ENRICH *the* LIVES *of* OTHERS

In reflecting back to 1978 when I began my professional career, I now realize that my pursuit of "success" would be much different if provided the opportunity for a "redo." Like all college graduates, I was highly driven to achieve success as the world defined it—power, authority, wealth and influence.

With the passage of 40 years, more gray hair, accomplishments and disappointments, I now realize that success looks much different to me today. My experience has taught me that it is more worthy to be "others focused" rather than "me focused."

I have now experienced the joy of making investments and working on projects for which I have a driving passion. The opportunity to work on ideas and projects that lead to long-term, sustainable benefits to others has taught me two key competencies for true success—servant leadership and humility. For that, I am grateful and hopeful that I can encourage young professionals to view their careers as an opportunity to enrich the lives of others—not just success for themselves. ★

GEORGE ROBERTS JR.
Northeast Texas Public Health District, CEO

George Roberts has served as the chief executive officer of the Northeast Texas Public Health District since November 2006.

Services provided by the health district include the Center for Healthy Living, community outreach, environmental health, immunizations, tuberculosis control, public health emergency preparedness, regional laboratory, vital statistics, and the WIC (Women, Infants and Children) Program. The health district primarily serves Tyler and Smith County but also provides some services in 21 counties in East Texas. The WIC Program serves a 20-county area, and Public Health Emergency Preparedness serves a seven-county region.

It's All About Relationships

So much of academic life revolves around classes, studies, projects and exams. During this time, you have had the opportunity to learn the one lesson that will prove invaluable to your future success: How to build and nurture positive relationships!

By now, you know the best way to get the most out of a class is to establish a relationship with your professor and to arrange for study sessions with classmates. I encourage you to take this same approach to your new job, bosses and colleagues.

Take an interest in your superiors and peers. Be intentional about communication through written notes (yes, handwritten notes), emails, texts and positive uplifting face-to-face contact to thank and encourage them. Then, carry these same techniques to your personal and professional relationships in the broader community. You never know who will be the connector to your next position.

Remain diligent, and your positive career growth will prove "it's all about relationships." ★

SMITTEE ROOT
Leadership Tyler, Executive Director

Smittee Root is the executive director for Leadership Tyler.

Leadership Tyler is a nonprofit organization serving the Tyler area by providing programs that focus on developing and equipping leaders to enrich the Tyler area community.

KEEP LEARNING

In my personal journey, the single most important thing that I can attribute to doing work that I love has been a relentless pursuit of continued learning.

The key is to be open to learning in different ways. Simply cultivating an attitude of curiosity has led me to read more, ask questions and to imagine bigger and better solutions not only in my work, but also in the world.

I continue to be amazed at how much there is to learn from others—both those who have come before me as well as young adults just beginning their own professional journeys. Realizing how much I don't know has made me more confident. That may seem counterintuitive, but there is a true sense of freedom in knowing that there is no real end to learning. ★

BOB ROSEMAN
Prothro, Wilhelmi & Co., PLLC, Partner

Bob Roseman joined Prothro, Wilhelmi and Co. in 2002 and became a partner in 2004. He has over 36 years of broad-based business experience, 19 of which were spent in industry primarily as a corporate executive. He has held positions as president and CEO, vice president for business development and corporate controller in public and privately held companies.

His practice includes audits, tax return preparation, consulting as an outsourced CFO/controller, mergers and acquisitions, strategic business forecasting and planning, tax strategy and executive coaching.

LIFE'S PURPOSE

I encourage you frequently to take the time to step back and assess where all your hard work fits into your overall purpose in life.

You have been blessed with very specific talents and gifts, which should serve to accomplish that purpose. When your purpose is clear, the hard work and determination is much easier along the way.

God, the creator of all things, including you, is the source of your unique gifts and talents. He will guide you toward the purpose.

My career as a CPA has been a rewarding journey that God has used to provide great influence and fulfillment. The relationships made and people served have provided the greatest joy along the way.

Seek God and His kingdom, adopt an attitude of gratitude, commit to excellence in all you do, and never be afraid of hard work. ★

BRYAN ROSSMAN
Tyler Adams Engineers & Development
Consultants, Principal and Director of Operations

Bryan Rossman has been part of the leadership team at Adams for over six years and is a valuable asset to the team because of his outstanding background in leadership, business operations and development services. In addition to his operational duties, Bryan utilizes his vast experience in business development, construction administration and owner's representation to expand the scope of consulting and development services offered by Adams Engineering.

Bryan leads a team of civil and environmental engineers and landscape architects in the Tyler office for Adams Engineering. He also leads development services (program management/ owner's representation) for both private market and public institutional clients.

KNOWLEDGE *and* UNDERSTANDING

I encourage you to consider your own career success as a work in progress—never-ending, always discovering new seasons of your career development.

Know that you will be a success if you apply knowledge and understanding to the many decisions you will make while defining your career. How much time you have invested in establishing your core values to influence decisions has much to do with achieving career success.

My foundational values, which affected my career decisions over the years, are faith, relationships and failure. Yes, failure, which I consider most valuable in my own career development.

You see, I experienced an epic career failure requiring a complete career change. After which, I learned to make decisions based on earned knowledge with applied understanding to achieve success beyond what I could ever have imagined.

Enjoy the challenge of your career development and all its valued experiences. ★

THE HONORABLE MATT SCHAEFER
Texas House of Representatives

Rep. Matt Schaefer is a sixth generation Texan and was first elected to the Texas House of Representatives, House District 6, in 2012. He also serves as a lieutenant commander in the U.S. Navy reserve and is self-employed in real estate and law.

The REAL MEASURE *of* SUCCESS

S uccess is measured by eternal principles, not worldly standards, and WHAT you do is not as important as WHY you do it.

I love that UT Tyler students are called Patriots because that helps us remember what made our nation great. Patriots of old knew our rights come from God, not government. I will paraphrase John Adams who wrote about our nation's success: "Our Constitution only works in a nation of people who value morality and spiritual truth." In other words, America is great when Americans are good.

Success is defined by honoring our fathers and mothers. Justice. Mercy. Humility. Integrity. It starts with families. Our nation desperately needs strong, successful families.

Success is much more than money. In fact, money is an unreliable indicator of success. Wisdom and understanding are more profitable than silver and gold. Chasing material things can lead to big trouble. Success involves patience and discipline. It is about getting it right on the things that truly matter. ★

MARK SEGUIN
*A Training and Risk Management Company,
Founder and CEO*

Mark Seguin is the founder of TBG Solutions
Inc., a risk management and training solutions
company that develops strategies, training and
awareness programs to keep staff, students
and employees safe. Mark's identity was stolen
as a child. Unfortunately, it went undetected
until adulthood. From this experience, Mark
recognized the rising rate of identity theft and
the devastating consequences.

These factors influenced Mark to build what is
now a cutting-edge, risk management training
and consulting company. He specializes in
training that brings about a change in behavior.
Mark has developed training on a variety of
topics from active shooter response options,
social media and identity theft awareness to
exceptional communication/customer
service training.

The PEOPLE *in* OUR LIVES

I was just a kid with little education and small hopes. My dream was average—to have a 9–5 job, a family, a house and a little retirement saved up when I am 65, but I didn't even know how to make that happen.

Then I heard, you are the sum-total of the five people with whom you surround yourself.

With that, I found others who had the success that I desired. My friend, Andy, encouraged me to quit my 9–5 and start using my skills shoeing horses. Jan-Harry encouraged me to take a big risk and purchase my first rent house. Stepp took me in, gave me a career test and devoted time helping me develop skills in sales and speaking.

You see, it is the people in our lives who are the biggest part of our success. If I didn't meet these people who saw something in me that I didn't see in myself, I would not be where I am today. It was their experience, insight and advice that inspired me to do more. ★

JO ANN SIMMONS, EdD
The University of Texas at Tyler University Academy Charter School, Superintendent

Dr. Jo Ann Simmons has served as superintendent of The University of Texas at Tyler University Academy, a T-STEM designated charter school, since October 2014. The charter serves around 725 students on three separate campuses.

She has worked in public education for the past 19 years. Prior to joining the University Academy, she served as principal at James S. Hogg Middle School and assistant principal at A.T. Stewart Middle School in Tyler Independent School District.

SMARTER *than* YOU

The best advice I have ever gotten was to hire people who are smarter than you are. Don't hire people from whom you cannot learn or people who do not challenge you.

This is very difficult for most leaders because our natural tendency is to worry about being outshined by a subordinate.

Effective leaders are comfortable enough with their own position that they hire people beneath them who are extraordinary. Too often, middle managers hire mediocre people beneath them in order to look good by comparison. According to research from the *Harvard Business Journal*, bad hiring decisions may account for up to 80 percent of employee turnover, and they usually could have been mitigated by choosing the smartest and most qualified candidate.

When you're making a personnel decision, I challenge you to select the candidate who may be the next CEO of the company. ★

JOHN SOULES SR.
John Soules Foods, Chairman

A native East Texan, John Soules is the founder and chairman of John Soules Foods Inc., the leading producer of beef and chicken fajitas in the United States, with a retail presence of more than 17,000 stores in 50 states.

John also is a steadfast supporter of Tyler and East Texas, giving generously of his time and resources to various community efforts.

It's All About *the* Team

Your success while in college, as in your career, will be the result of the "team" you join, support and utilize. Teams often consists of family, co-workers, mentors and friends—those people who help shine a light on your path to success. Entering college, you are suddenly given the opportunity for a great team resource—advisors, professors, social groups, study groups, etc.

You will play a major role in your achievements, but appreciate the fact that others will contribute as well. No single individual accomplishes everything alone. Therefore, I encourage you to carefully develop, support and appreciate your team because they multiply your efforts as well as your successes.

Great things in business are never accomplished by one person. They are the result of a great team. Aristotle said it best: "The whole is greater than the sum of its parts." ★

TODD STAPLES
Texas Oil and Gas Association, President

Todd Staples was named president of the Texas
Oil and Gas Association in 2014. As president
of the state's oldest and largest trade association
representing the industry, Todd has focused
on expanding TXOGA's presence as the "go-
to" source for reliable and credible oil and gas
information. In order to continue a positive job
and growth environment that oil and natural gas
provides for Texas, TXOGA must be a modern-
day voice for the industry.

Prior to TXOGA, he served as the Texas
agriculture commissioner, winning two
statewide elections. He also served with
distinction in the Texas Senate and Texas
House of Representatives.

Strong Values

There's a common saying associated with success, "If you just believe, you can achieve." However, if it were that simple, everybody would be Bill Gates.

While there's no roadmap to success or even a unanimous definition for the word itself, the values that define you and orient your choices can act as a compass, pointing you toward your future and toward what success looks like for you.

Developing a lasting value system to guide you requires more than just a vision. It requires hard work and sacrifice, and lots of it.

Make each responsibility a personal challenge to go out and perform to your best ability every day. The challenges change, but the blueprint that is your values will help you meet all of them, and if your values are strong, your future will be as well. ★

THE HONORABLE BILL STOUDT
Gregg County, Texas, County Judge

Judge Bill Stoudt has served as the Gregg County judge since 2003. He is a member of the Texas Association of Counties, Gregg County Bail Bond Board and the Longview Rotary Club. He founded the Boys & Girls Club of East Texas and the Centurion Club.

He is chairman of the I-20 East Texas Corridor Advisory Committee, East Texas Council of Governments and the Gregg County Juvenile Board, and he is a community advisor for the Junior League of Longview. Additionally, he is a former director and former chairman of the Longview Economic Development Corp., Gregg County Appraisal District, city of Longview Higher Education Council, Cherokee Water Company and Regions Bank. Stoudt received a Bachelor of Business Administration from Georgia State University. Judge Stoudt is currently serving as chairman of the State Commission on Jail Standards.

Honor Your Commitments

One of the things my dad told me when I was younger, and it has always stuck with me, is only you can give your handshake away.

The handshake is one of the highest forms of symbolic currency. By not honoring your handshake and your word, you have in essence given it away. If you make a bad deal in business, and you gave your handshake, you need to honor it and learn from the mistake.

When you commit to something, make sure you did not give your handshake in vain. ★

ELAM SWANN
Swann Furniture & Design, CEO

Elam Swann presides over Swann Furniture & Design, a family business that has been serving the Tyler area for more than 120 years.

He joined the company in 1975 as a salesman, and by 1980, he assumed management responsibilities. Since that time, he has guided the growth of the company, which included moving to new locations and expanding the services offered.

The FUNDAMENTAL PRINCIPLES

As you contemplate your time at UT Tyler, you might ask yourself, Where do I start? What path should I follow? What should my goals be? When considering these questions, many of your fundamental principles will remain the same. These principles will carry you through every stage of your life, creating a "road map" to help you "thrive" in all you do.

Begin and end each day asking for guidance and clarity through prayer. Think as a leader. Live with unwavering integrity. Choose your friends carefully. Learn continuously. Make smart daily choices. Think outside the box. Stay healthy with a daily workout routine and diet. And find a solid mentor that can help you answer "the hard questions."

You have one life. It's a gift. Live it well! ★

JIMMY TOLER
Tyler Police Department, Chief

Jimmy Toler is a 25-year veteran of the Tyler Police Department. As the chief of police, he commands a department comprised of 248 employees (196 Sworn) and oversees an annual operating budget of $27 million.

Chief Toler began his career with the Tyler Police Department in 1993. During his years of service with the department, he had the opportunity to work within the patrol, investigations and administrative divisions. Prior to being promoted, he worked as a patrol officer, youth crimes investigator, crimes against children investigator and district investigator.

Opportunities

I have always operated under a simple philosophy: Take advantage of opportunities when they present themselves. Trust the process and leave every assignment or position in a better state than you found it.

You should never pass up an opportunity because you are afraid to try new things or take risks. Others often see skills and abilities in you, and they believe that you are the right person for an assignment or position, even when you do not.

Fast-tracking growth will not work for everyone, so it is essential to set a steady pace with defined goals of improvement. This belief in steady growth and continuous improvement has guided me throughout my professional career. ★

SASHA VUKELJA, MD/FACP
Texas Oncology, Oncologist

An oncologist at the Tyler Cancer Center, Dr. Sasha Vukelja is deeply involved in the holistic care of her patients, forming several support groups. She was instrumental in bringing the Susan G. Komen Race for the Cure to Tyler, and she is the founding member of the Women's Fund.

While she has written three books and is presently writing her fourth, she is best known for her ministry, Church Under the Bridge, where she is working to build a chapel for the homeless called This Little Light of Mine.

Just *a* Few Things

Education is like a passport. It will take you places. Live, live, live, do not just exist. Live as you may live forever. Behave as if you may die tomorrow.

Art is a medicine and medicine is an art. We all have a light inside of us. Let your light shine so that you make a difference, not just a living.

In the words of Denver Moore, "You can't help everybody, but everybody can help somebody."

You don't have to have a million dollars to help someone or wait for something big to happen before you help. Just do something, because what you do may mean the world to one person. It can be something small, such as helping with errands or something as simple as a smile. Let someone know that you care in a world where a lot of people don't care. ★

KEN WAITS
Mewbourne Oil Co., CEO

Kenneth S. Waits received his BS in petroleum engineering from the University of Oklahoma (OU) in 1983 and did graduate business work at UT Tyler in 1988. Upon graduation, he joined Mewbourne Oil Co. as a drilling engineer, and after serving in various roles, Ken was promoted to vice president in 1996 and president in 2010. He now serves as the president and CEO of Mewbourne Oil Co., one of the largest and most successful independent oil and gas companies in America. He has been active in numerous industry and community organizations, as well as a long time supporter of OU. Ken and his wife of 30 years, Laura Waits, reside in Tyler, Texas. They are the proud parents of Hanna Waits, a freshman at OU.

Embracing Challenges

I have been fortunate to have a front row seat to observe and learn from some incredibly successful people—entrepreneurs, CEOs of major oil companies, politicians and other very powerful people. The lessons I have learned from them are what inspire me and would be the advice I would give to UT Tyler students.

My counsel would be this: It may take time, but find work about which you are passionate. Not everybody finds his or her dream job on day one!

Once you do, recognize that regardless of the job you have or the industry you are in, trials and tribulations will come. I encourage you to embrace these challenging times and recognize that amidst the trials, there is opportunity. Challenging times are full of risk, volatility and uncertainty, which will paralyze many people, but successful people recognize them as their friend. It's in these times, we have the opportunity to differentiate ourselves. It won't be easy, in fact, it will require tremendous perseverance. We all get knocked down, but those who have the will and courage to keep getting back up, will be the most successful. ★

DON WARREN
Councilman for City of Tyler; Lomoco Inc.,
President and Owner

Don Warren is the owner and president of Lomoco Inc., a small oil and gas asset management firm, which he formed in 1994. He has been an oil and gas professional for the last 36 years.

Standing *on a* Tricycle Seat Flapping *my* Wings

Over 50 years ago while attending kindergarten, I was asked to participate in a Thanksgiving pageant, and my job was to dress up and act like a turkey. I had beautiful wings made of feathers and a long beak that attached to my nose.

The afternoon after the pageant, I had a brilliant idea. Wearing my turkey wings, I went out into my front yard and stood on my red tricycle seat flapping my wings as hard as I could. I jumped off my tricycle seat and tried to fly.

I tried repeatedly until it finally sank in that I would not be able to fly. That was over 50 years ago, yet I remember it like it was just yesterday.

Throughout my entire life, there have been difficulties and significant challenges. I have always made a personal and professional choice to persevere and not let bumps in the road get me down. Just like 50 years ago, I continue to stand on my tricycle seat and flap my wings. You never achieve success and happiness by just sitting on your seat and not pursuing your dreams. ★

THE HONORABLE JAMES T. WORTHEN
12th Court of Appeals, Chief Justice

Chief Justice James Worthen practiced law in Tyler from 1980–1998, initially with the partnership of Sammons and Parker, then with the firm of Bain, Files, Worthen and Jarrett, PC. He served the State of Texas as a justice on the 12th Court of Appeals in Tyler from 1999–2002 and became its chief justice in 2003. Chief Justice Worthen served as chairman of the Council of Chief Justices 2005–2006.

He is author of *The Organizational and Structural Development of Intermediate Appellate Courts in Texas, 1892–2003* published in *South Texas Law Review, Fall, 2004*.

A UT Tyler alum, Chief Justice Worthen holds Bachelor of Science and Master of Arts degrees.

Weekly Success

Early in my career, I read an article describing what separates success from failure. The author's most important factor was what you were doing at 9 p.m. Sunday night. Successful individuals were actively planning what they would be doing during the upcoming week to further their job and career. Although it may be your style to do this at 8 p.m. or 10 p.m., it is important to be prepared for the upcoming week.

Those who "fail to plan, plan to fail." When you have successful week after successful week as you go through your career, you will be a success.

The late Jack Kemp, who was a professional quarterback, congressman and member of President George H.W. Bush's cabinet, was once asked about his success in life. He responded that when he continued to make first downs, the touchdowns would come.

Keep making first downs on a weekly basis, and you will be pleased with your score. ★

Topical Index